Applied Creative Followership™
A Guide to Beginning Your Journey

Michael Cooley
With
Jimmy Collins

Creative Followership, LLC

Contents

Point of View	6
Introduction	7
Instructions	9
Study Pages	11
Self-Made Principles	55

Applied Creative Followership
Point of View

STOP!

Do not go past this page without understanding our unique perspective. We approach things differently than most authors of leadership books.

Applied Creative Followership is presented from the follower's point of view not from the leader's.

The application of Creative Followership and the benefits of its practice are presented only from the follower's point of view because we want the reader to clearly understand the relationship. There is not a shortage of material available from the leader's point of view, but there is virtually nothing from the follower's viewpoint.

Creative Followership exists to illustrate the unlimited opportunities the practice of the Principles of Creative Followership offers both dedicated followers and potential followers, and inspire them to choose the path of Creative Followership for their journey to that destination we all seek — success and satisfaction.

For those who think of themselves being leaders, rather than followers, we would like to remind you that everyone has one or more persons to whom they are accountable. The department head in an organization has a boss, the CEO reports to a board of directors, even the president of the United States has checks and balances from the other branches of government and the voting public. Therefore, everyone is at one time or another, in some way or another a follower regardless of title, position, status, or personal wealth or accomplishments in life.

We realize all followers report to a boss and that the boss may or may not be a leader. We hope that all Creative Followers will, at some point in their career, find a leader worthy of their talent, experience, creativity and followership.

Effectively practiced, Creative Followership will create a relationship of mutual trust and support between the follower and the leader.

We invite you to become a Creative Follower.

Introduction

There are many different opinions about how to be successful. One of the most prevalent notions claims that your ambition and positive attitude capture all the necessary ingredients you need to get ahead in business and in your career. "Do whatever it takes," "Be a leader," "Lead from the front," or even, "Be a Servant Leader," are some of the most popular mantras often repeated by those in the leadership development industry.

In reality, the slogans of the call to leadership fail because not everyone can be a leader; not everyone will be a leader; not everyone will have authority over others. If you seek an alternative to the worn out slogans of the leadership development industry, you have come to the right place. Here you will not find leadership training but something called Creative Followership. Creative Followership will change the way you approach your boss, your coworkers, and your career.

Applied Creative Followership is based on the book *Creative Followership: In the Shadow of Greatness*, by Jimmy Collins. Creative Followership is not just another book on leadership. Instead, it is designed to offer you a process for achieving success in your career. Written from the perspective of the follower instead of the leader, you will learn principles everyone can apply regardless of your position in the organization.

One word of caution: you cannot become a Creative

Follower from just reading a book. You can, however, become a Creative Follower by engaging in the process of applying the Principles of Creative Followership on your own, inventing your own principles, and then re-visiting the process to reinvent yourself again and again.

It is my hope that this workbook facilitates your journey and increases your opportunity to think about several of the key principles of Creative Followership. Take this time to confront the false assumptions, the prevailing myths, and then contrast them with the principles of Creative Followership. Rethink how and why we choose role models and how we define leadership and followers.

Creative Followership will not be just me talking to you. Rather than a one-way conversation, you will have the opportunity to use your voice to engage the material and comment yourself. Just as *Creative Followership* does not conform to the mold of traditional business books, *Applied Creative Followership* is not your typical workbook. This study is not designed to lead you to a set of predetermined answers or conclusions. As with any guided program of study, you will get as much as you are willing to give. If you invest time and study in both texts, you will be more equipped for the exciting journey into Creative Followership.

Instructions

The more effort and thought you give the principles addressed in this book, the more you will get out of it. To help you in your journey to discovering Creative Followership, here are some tips for using this workbook.

FIRST THINGS FIRST
Read the chapters that correlate to each study session. If you've read the book straight through, give the chapter for your current study time a second look. Keep it handy, in case you want to look back. Use these books side by side so you can use my thoughts to shape your own.

ALONE OR TOGETHER
Applied Creative Followership can be a singular journey or a shared journey. You can take these study sessions one at a time on your own, or you can go through them with a group of like-minded colleagues. Working through this book with a group will open your mind to thoughts and ideas you might not have discovered on your own, but even if you do go through this book with a group, I would encourage you to answer the questions on your own in advance, so you can give them proper time.

SPEAKING OF TIME
Don't cram. Don't rush. Whether you do one a day or one a week, give yourself time to think through these lessons and really apply them to yourself.

FALSE ASSUMPTIONS
Each session begins with a False Assumption that most people have toward work. The goal of each session is to counter that assumption with one of the principles of Creative Followership. Take a moment to reflect on the assumption and the principle. How does the principle change the way you view work?

CREATIVE FOLLOWERSHIP PRINCIPLE

False Assumptions are followed by Principles of Creative Followership that are found in the book. The chapter is referenced in parentheses.

DISCOVERING CREATIVE FOLLOWERSHIP

The Assumptions and Principles are followed by a series of questions intended to help you think deeper about that principle. Take each question one at a time. Write your answers down in your own words. Be as brief or as detailed as you feel necessary, but above all, be honest!

FOLLOW UP

Don't let the end of this workbook be the end of your thought process on Creative Followership. Spend time following up with your study mates. Revisit the book and the workbook. Track your progress in becoming a Creative Follower and revisit the answers you wrote down.

Think about your personal development and discover new ways you can fulfill the role of a Creative Follower not mentioned in the book. As you engage the material, you will have your own thoughts and suggestions about Creative Followership. When that happens, take a minute to capture your ideas by writing them down at the bottom of the page. You will be able to use these notes after you complete the study pages.

How has Creative Followership changed you? How has your perspective on Creative Followership changed? What can you do to further tweak your approach to work and pursue your goals?

PART 1
THE PHILOSOPHY OF FOLLOWERSHIP

Study 1

False Assumption: I must find a successful role model to learn how to be a successful leader

Creative Followership: Never try to be a copy of anyone else. It never works. It is easy to believe we can find someone successful and mirror his or her behavior and be successful too. Imitations always end up being less desirable than the original. Being authentic will bring you more success than being a replica of someone else. (From Chapter 1)

Applied Creative Followership:

1. More than likely, we have all tried to imitate people we admire. Who have you looked up to and tried to imitate?

2. Think about your strengths and talents and how you can use those to do the things you really enjoy. List those abilities you believe help you succeed.

3. Why is it important for you to be you?

4. How might a part-time job or internship help someone who is a student learn his or her strengths and career preferences?

Study 2

False Assumption: There is a multitude of ways to define Leadership. One of the most popular says, "Leadership is influence."

Creative Followership: A leader is someone who has followers. (From Chapter 2)

Applied Creative Followership:

1. Consider Jimmy's definition of a leader. Do you agree or disagree with this definition?

2. How does Jimmy's definition of a leader affect your understanding of leadership and who you consider a leader?

3. Do you consider yourself a leader? Why or why not?

4. Why would Jimmy think leadership is something more than influence? Use his definition of leadership to formulate an answer.

5. How does Jimmy's definition of leadership change your perspective or your thoughts about leadership?

Study 3

False Assumption: Being a follower makes one a subservient person who does everything the boss says. People want to be leaders not followers.

Creative Followership: Creative followers are dynamic, intelligent, and creative people who join in partnership with a leader around a common purpose, goal, or objective. Being in the "shadow" of a leader is not a subservient place but a wise position to place oneself. (From Chapters 2 and 3)

Applied Creative Followership:

1. Being a follower gets a bad rap. When you hear the idea of being a "follower," what negative ideas do you immediately think?

2. Why should you examine the "shadow" of a person before choosing him or her as your boss?

3. How would you evaluate a potential boss?

4. A follower is united with a leader in pursuit of a unifying purpose. What kind of "purpose" do you think you could advocate?

Study 4

False Assumption: Some companies are just lousy places to work. If you work for one, you ought to leave and find employment somewhere else.

Creative Followership: You can fire your boss if you have a lousy one. You can and do have the ability to choose your boss. (From Chapter 4)

Principle #1 – Choose Your Boss

Applied Creative Followership:

1. What does Jimmy mean when he says he "fired his boss?"

2. Under what circumstances would Jimmy advise someone to fire their boss?

3. What four criteria did Jimmy determine he would look for in a boss?

Study 5

False Assumption: Leaders lead from the front, and those who follow come behind them. The followers wait to be told what to do and how to do it. The leader sets the pace for others to fall in line.

Creative Followership: Look for and find a boss who will allow you to be creative and express yourself. (From Chapter 5)

Applied Creative Followership:

1. What does Jimmy mean when he describes the importance of working for a leader who allows followers to "express themselves?"

2. How important is it to you to be able to express yourself and execute tasks or complete projects using your own ideas?

PART 2:
THE PRINCIPLES OF FOLLOWERSHIP

Study 6

False Assumption: You can't learn anything profitable from a lousy boss. It is best just to move on as quickly as possible.

Creative Followership: Your life and career are a journey; you can learn from both the lousy bosses and the best bosses. (From Chapter 6)

Applied Creative Followership:

1. What does Jimmy mean when he says most followers are first hired as workers and then become followers?

2. How can you "learn" from a lousy boss?

3. How can you "learn" from a good boss?

Study 7

False Assumption: Just do what you are told to do, and do not question or overthink the tasks and projects you have to complete. Just get it done like you are told to do it.

Creative Followership: You should know your boss's strengths, weaknesses, what he or she likes to do and what he or she does not like to do. (From Chapter 6)

Principle #2 – Know Your Boss

Applied Creative Followership:

1. Why does Jimmy advocate getting to know your boss?

2. How would you accomplish the task of getting to know your boss?

3. Why would some people be afraid to apply this principle?

Study 8

False Assumption: Some bosses are lazy and there's nothing you can do about it. You have to work around them and hope for the best on your performance evaluation.

Creative Followership: You should be thankful for a "do-nothing" boss. The opportunities are endless. (From Chapter 6)

Principle #3 – Do What Your Boss Does Not Like To Do

Applied Creative Followership:

1. Why would Jimmy say we ought to be thankful for a "do-nothing" boss?

2. How does principle #2 "Know Your Boss" appear to be the logical first step before principle #3 "Do What Your Boss Does Not Like To Do?"

3. How would you as a manager, with positional authority over several workers, respond to a worker who found the things you did not like to do and completed these tasks with excellence?

Study 9

False Assumption: My boss does not have the skills to do several aspects of his or her job well. There is nothing I can do about my boss's shortcomings.

Creative Followership: I can become invaluable to my boss if I can complete some of the tasks he or she does not do well. (From Chapter 6)

Principle #4 – Do What Your Boss Does Not Do Well

Applied Creative Followership:

1. How would you begin doing the things your boss does not do well?

2. How will your boss react if you begin doing one or more of those things your boss does not do well?

3. How important is it to make sure you complete what is expected of you before attempting to do additional tasks for your boss?

4. Can you think of one thing you might accomplish on behalf of your boss in order to get this process started?

Study 10

False Assumption: In order to advance my career, I must do whatever is necessary to stand out, get noticed, and get ahead. It's OK if I do things better than my boss and get the credit.

Creative Followership: It is better to avoid attention-getting performance and not get into a competition with your boss. (From Chapter 6)

Principle #5 – Do Not Compete With Your Boss

Applied Creative Followership:

1. Why would it be better to avoid getting into a position of competition with your boss?

2. How can you apply Principle #4 – Do What Your Boss Does Not Do Well and not violate Principle #5 – Do Not Compete With Your Boss?

3. If you apply Principle #5 – Do Not Compete With Your Boss, will it hold your career back or advance it forward?

Study 11

False Assumption: I will advance my career if I make sure I get all the credit for my work, my suggestions, and my success stories. I must put my best foot forward and make sure I look good to the decision makers in the organization.

Creative Followership: It is better to make my boss look good than make myself look good. This is the path to real advancement and job security. (From Chapter 6)

Principle #6 – Make Your Boss Look Good

Applied Creative Followership:

1. Do you have to "like" your boss in order to make him or her "look good?"

2. What does Jimmy mean when he writes, "You are a volunteer?"

3. How can making a lousy boss look good benefit your career advancement?

Study 12

False Assumption: A person works to gain recognized authority and a title to back it up. Gaining recognition and authority are signs of success in a person's career.

Creative Followership: Do not wait for more authority or ask for more responsibility; just take more responsibility. (From Chapter 7)

Principle #7 – Take Responsibility

Applied Creative Followership:

1. Do you think it is true when you want more responsibility at work, that it is simply there for the taking?

2. How are responsibility and authority linked together?

Study 13

False Assumption: No one likes to deal with problems. You are more likely to succeed in your career if you take on projects and tasks where you are more likely to gain a "win." Leave the difficult and risky for someone else.

Creative Followership: Problems should be viewed as adventures and challenges, and one should think about the satisfaction gained from solving a problem using creativity and initiative. (From Chapter 7)

Principle #8 – Everyone Likes Problems

Applied Creative Followership:

1. Describe the problem you had the most fun solving at work.

2. What does Jimmy mean when he says bosses like to pick and choose their problems?

3. What is the best way to turn a problem around and think of it as an opportunity to show the boss what you can do?

Study 14

False Assumption: Protect your authority and your territory at work. If you let up, you will lose ground to coworkers, and surrendered ground is the hardest to recapture. Be alert to those who challenge your area of responsibility.

Creative Followership: Responsibility is gained when you take it; the more responsibility and authority you gain, the less time you will have for some tasks in your area you are accustomed to doing. Release these tasks to others in order to free yourself in an effort to gain new and different responsibilities. (From Chapter 7)

Principle #9 – Do Not Hoard Authority

Applied Creative Followership:

1. How can you avoid the temptation to hoard authority?

2. What are some of the dangers of marking off and defending your "territory" in your area of responsibility?

3. Why is it beneficial for you to release responsibility to others who are willing to take it?

4. What should you do if you discover you have overstepped your boundaries and caused friction between you and the boss or coworkers—or both?

Study 15

False Assumption: People who push the envelope of their authority are troublemakers. We ought to discourage people from overstepping the boundaries of their job descriptions and infringing on the territory of others. Everyone has a job description and everyone should stay within the boundaries of the clearly defined lines of responsibility.

Creative Followership: People who take initiative and live on the edge of their authority are bound to step over the line occasionally. People who take chances are more valuable to an organization than those who are difficult to motivate. (From Chapter 7)

Principle #10 – It Is Better to Restrain Mustangs than Kick Mules

Applied Creative Followership:
1. What type of people do you prefer to work with? "Mules" or "Mustangs?" Why?

2. Do you consider yourself a "Mustang" or a "Mule?"

3. Are you a "Mustang" at heart, but up until now you have been lacking in the courage to step out and test the boundaries of your responsibility? How can you break out and begin pushing the envelope at work?

Study 16

False Assumption: If I know how to get the job done, I ought to be able to complete tasks and projects my way, even if that means doing them in a different manner than I was told to do them.

Creative Followership: You have to find the balance between what is expected of you and what is efficient. Treat tasks and assignments like a collaboration between you and the boss, realizing the boss has the final say in whether you have met expectations or not. (From Chapter 7)

Principle #11 – Do It the Way the Boss Likes It Done

Applied Creative Followership:

1. Is there a line between independent creativity and following instructions?

2. How can you find ways to be creative within the boundaries of the boss's wishes without damaging the intent or outcome of the goal?

3. What are the limitations of your level of independence?

Study 17

False Assumption: If you disagree with a decision the boss has made, make it known, so you can separate yourself from the boss's decision. It's OK to stand out and disagree with the boss.

Creative Followership: Make your actions and the boss's virtually indistinguishable; disagree with the boss in private, but in public, stand in unison with the boss's decision. (From Chapter 7)

Principle #12 – Let Others See the Boss in You

Applied Creative Followership:

1. How does Jimmy say he handled situations where he disagreed with a decision Truett had made?

2. How can you make your work mirror the quality and character of the boss?

3. Why is it important to do things that meet and exceed the boss's expectations?

Study 18

False Assumption: It is most important that I advance my career. I do not need to worry about helping the boss.

Creative Followership: Discover ways to help your boss advance his or her career. Your career advancement will follow if you make yourself valuable to your boss. (From Chapter 7)

Principle #13 – Help Your Boss Succeed

Applied Creative Followership:

1. How can you help your boss?

2. What kind of employee are you? Does your boss think you are helpful and have his or her best interest in mind?

3. Why is it important to help your boss succeed?

4. Why would it be important to think about your co-workers as you do things to help your boss succeed?

Study 19

False Assumption: Reveal your innovative ideas when you have the opportunity to share them in a large group setting. You will have maximum exposure and get full credit for your creativity.

Creative Followership: It is better to work at getting people to buy-in and get their advice on your ideas in advance. (From Chapter 7)

Principle #14 – Build Support in Advance

Applied Creative Followership:

1. Why does Jimmy advocate approaching those in authority who might oppose your ideas before a presentation?

2. Why do you think it is important to get people to buy-in before major announcements or sharing new or innovative ideas about the business?

Study 20

False Assumption: If the boss wants something done, or proposes a new policy or procedure, it is my duty to comply. If the plan is not well thought-out, that's the boss's fault. The boss doesn't really get concerned about what I think.

Creative Followership: The role of a Creative Follower demands constant evaluation and monitoring of what happens in the organization. Followers use that information to help the boss succeed and to assist others in the organization to fully understand the role they play within new initiatives and the unifying purpose of the organization. (From Chapter 8)

Principle #15 – Gather, Interpret, Translate, Repackage

Applied Creative Followership:

1. How can you assist the boss in assimilating information throughout the organization?

2. What does Jimmy mean when he says people in different departments in the organization see specifics and details of new initiatives through "different lenses?"

3. Explain why "humor" and a "smile" are essential to the delivery when you repackage a message from the boss.

4. Explain the role of the Creative Follower in repackaging negative feedback.

Study 21

False Assumption: It is more beneficial to hear praise and encouraging words than it is to hear negative comments about your work or performance.

Creative Followership: Seek reliable and authentic negative feedback; it is the only type of feedback that produces change and improvement. (From Chapter 8)

Principle #16 – The Only Real Feedback Is Negative

Applied Creative Followership:

1. Why is positive feedback less valuable than negative feedback according to Jimmy?

2. Why is it important that negative feedback be specific?

3. What role can you play in providing specific negative feedback for the boss?

4. Explain why a Creative Follower who provides authentic negative feedback is an asset to the boss and the organization.

Study 22

False Assumption: People who criticize specific qualities in the processes and procedures spread negativity and ought to be avoided.

Creative Followership: Invite complaints, dissent, and negative feedback. (From Chapter 8)
Principle #17 – Cultivate Feedback

Applied Creative Followership:
1. How does Jimmy describe his process of cultivating negative feedback?

2. How must the Creative Follower learn to view his or her own negative feedback?

3. Why is negative feedback from employees more valuable than surveys, comment cards, and focus groups?

Study 23

False Assumption: Ask customers if they enjoyed their experience with your company. This question provides valuable feedback of the organization's performance.

Creative Followership: Invite usable feedback by asking customers for suggestions about improvements rather than criticism. (From Chapter 8)

Principle #18 – Ask for Suggestions Rather than Criticism

Applied Creative Followership:

1. How is Jimmy's approach to asking for suggestions different from simple questions about satisfaction?

2. How much extra effort is involved in asking for suggestions?

3. What is the appropriate and best response to the customer's suggestions, both positive and negative?

Study 24

False Assumption: You have the right to explain yourself and your actions, especially if you are falsely accused of wrongdoing, negligence, or poor performance.

Creative Followership: The details as to why or how the problem occurred in a situation are less important than how you will exceed expectations through your solution to the issue. (From Chapter 8)

Principle #19 – Always Apologize, Never Explain

Applied Creative Followership:
1. How can you turn problems into opportunities?

2. Why would a boss or customer not be impressed with the way you defend yourself, your coworker(s) or your company when a problem occurs?

3. How can you use a bad situation to exceed expectations and make your boss or customer pleased with your resolution of a problem?

Study 25

False Assumption: Grumbling and negative comments about the boss and the organization are going to happen. You might as well listen and/or contribute. It helps people let off steam.

Creative Followership: Creative Followers do not have the time or patience to tolerate grumbling and murmuring; they understand how to execute the important role they play in stopping it. (From Chapter 8)
Principle #20 – Confront Grumbling and Murmuring

Applied Creative Followership:
1. How do you distinguish between grumbling and murmuring and constructive negative feedback?

2. What ways does Jimmy suggest for confronting people who grumble?

3. What positive suggestion can a Creative Follower give to a person who murmurs?

Study 26

False Assumption: My boss does not have the time or the interest in hearing what I think about his or her performance on the job. The boss really does not care what I think. The boss gets encouragement from upper management.

Creative Followership: Truett Cathy said, "Do you know how to tell if someone needs encouragement? They are breathing!" Bosses need encouragement just like the rest of us. (From Chapter 8)

Principle #21 – Encourage Your Boss

Applied Creative Followership:

1. Why does Jimmy think it is a good idea to encourage your boss?

2. Does your current boss receive enough encouragement?

3. How can you tactfully and earnestly encourage your boss?

Study 27

False Assumption: It is critical to learn the skills of making the best decisions and sort through the pros and cons of all available options.

Creative Followership: Worry less about how to make good decisions and more about making your decisions good. (From Chapter 9)
Principle #22 – Make Your Decisions Good

Applied Creative Followership:
1. Why does Jimmy think the issue is not about making good decisions but about making your decisions turn out well?

2. How can you "make a decision good"?

Study 28

False Assumption: People who consider themselves "followers" are passive, subservient, and lack the confidence necessary to lead and succeed.

Creative Followership: Creative Followers are not passive but assertive. (From Chapter 9)

Principle #23 – Be Assertive

Applied Creative Followership:

1. How does Jimmy define assertiveness? Do you agree or disagree with his definition? Explain your answer.

2. Is assertiveness dependent upon your feelings? Why or why not?

3. People who lack assertiveness make up for it in other ways. What examples does Jimmy give for the tactics of non-assertive people?

4. Explain what Jimmy means when he writes about the importance of being able to "assume a role."

Study 29

False Assumption: Opportunities are critically important; take advantage of every one that comes your way.

Creative Followership: Saying "no" can be the most beneficial word in the vocabulary of a Creative Follower. (From Chapter 9)

Principle #24 – Learn to Say No

Applied Creative Followership:

1. What does Jimmy mean when he says the word "no" protects the integrity of the unifying purpose, the leader, and benefits the organization?

2. What does Jimmy think is necessary for one's ability to be confidently assertive?

Study 30

False Assumption: Get it done; that's the most important thing.

Creative Followership: Whatever you do, make certain you do it the right way. (From Chapter 10)
Principle #25 – Do It Right

Applied Creative Followership:
1. How important to your reputation is the quality of your work?

2. What do you think of the following saying? "Any job worth doing is worth doing right."

Study 31

False Assumption: A model employee does what the job description requires.

Creative Followership: There is benefit in going above and beyond the call of duty. (From Chapter 10)

Principle #26 – Do More Than Is Expected

Applied Creative Followership:

1. What would happen if you were to take on more responsibility at work?

2. Is it possible to assume tasks and projects without asking permission?

3. What can you do to go above and beyond the call of duty and do more than is expected at work?

Study 32

False Assumption: Do what you're told to do at work. Do not make extra work for yourself before it is necessary.

Creative Followership: Take every opportunity you can to exceed expectations. Do not sit around waiting for an assignment; create assignments and get things done. (From Chapter 10)

Principle #27 – Do Not Wait To Be Told What To Do

Applied Creative Followership:

1. What are some repetitive tasks at work that you could perform "ahead of time?"

2. Are there other non-repetitive tasks at work that if you took the initiative to get done would be appreciated by the boss?

3. Why do you think your boss would highly value an employee that got things done without being asked?

Study 33

False Assumption: Avoid dirty and difficult jobs. There's no reason to put yourself out there and do work that is unpleasant.

Creative Followership: The boss is going to notice who is doing the dirty jobs, without any reminders, that no one else wants to do. (From Chapter 10)

Principle #28 – Do the Dirty and Difficult Jobs

Applied Creative Followership:

1. Jimmy says that the boss will notice the employees who take on the most unpleasant tasks. Do you think this is true? Why or why not?

2. How do you think this principle relates to Principle #26 - Do More Than Is Expected?

Study 34

False Assumption: Avoid drawing too much attention to yourself and make sure you do your job within the boundaries of your authority and job description.

Creative Followership: Do not be timid. If you see something that needs to be done, go ahead and do it. (From Chapter 10)

Principle #29 – Take Risks

Applied Creative Followership:

1. Explain what Jimmy means when he writes, "You do not need to fail in order to grow, but failure could be a good experience that will stimulate growth and future success."

2. What do you do if you take a risk at work and something goes wrong?

Study 35

False Assumption: If there is bad news at work, let someone else tell the boss the bad news.

Creative Followership: The sooner you report bad news and assist in finding a resolution the better the outcome will be. (From Chapter 10)

Principle #30 – Bad News Does Not Improve With Age

Applied Creative Followership:

1. Why is it better not to delay telling the boss bad news?

2. Why is it easier to talk about telling the boss bad news immediately than it is to actually tell the boss bad news?

3. Can you think of a time when a delay in information about a minor incident caused a larger catastrophe? How could the prompt delivery of information have avoided more issues?

Study 36

False Assumption: Personal discouragement is tough. It can drag you down and affect your performance.

Creative Followership: Learning how to overcome discouragement can help you out in difficult times. (From Chapter 11)

Principle #31 – Do Not Be Easily Discouraged

Applied Creative Followership:

1. What are some ways you can creatively overcome discouragement and not allow it to affect your performance?

2. Describe the benefits of learning to overcome discouragement.

Study 37

False Assumption: Critical people are just mean-spirited and/or jealous; there is no value in listening to what they say.

Creative Followership: Critical people offer you a priceless opportunity to test and clarify your position. (From Chapter 11)

Principle #32 – Be Thankful for Strong-Willed Critics

Applied Creative Followership:

1. Why does Jimmy say strong-willed critics provide an opportunity for personal growth?

2. What benefit could you gain by listening to criticism about your performance?

3. Why does learning to appreciate strong-willed criticism from others make you more valuable to the organization?

Study 38

False Assumption: There are times when you can lose valuable time and waste energy by unnecessarily "double checking" facts, figures, or other information. It is more productive to apply yourself to getting the task completed.

Creative Followership: It is wise to always verify as much information as you can. (From Chapter 11)

Principle #33 – Never Assume What You Can Verify

Applied Creative Followership:
1. Why is it important to double-check information?

2. Have you ever assumed something you could have verified?

3. How much additional time does it actually take to verify facts and figures?

Study 39

False Assumption: Good employees can simply listen to what you have to say and execute what you have said with excellence.

Creative Followership: People respond better if they can both hear and see what you are talking about. Creative Followers use ingenuity and provide their hearers with a tangible way to remember the message. (From Chapter 11)

Principle #34 – Use Actions and Symbols

Applied Creative Followership:

1. What and why are Creative Followers trying to communicate with others in the organization?

2. Why do actions and symbols enhance the communication process?

3. Where did Jimmy say he found inspiration for finding meaningful symbols?

4. Why is a dedicated and loyal Creative Follower so valuable to a leader?

Study 40

False Assumption: If you have a successful career and have achieved privileged status, you should enjoy everything you are offered. You have earned it; it's yours, so enjoy it while you can.

Creative Followership: The special privileges of an executive did not get you where you are in the organization; avoid them because you don't need them to be successful. (From Chapter 11)

Principle #35 – Avoid Executive Privilege

Applied Creative Followership:

1. What positive result does Jimmy say one gains from avoiding executive privilege?

2. What effect does avoiding executive privilege have on the morale of the organization?

3. What type of negative effects does enjoying the benefits of executive privilege have on the executive?

APPLYING CREATIVE FOLLOWERSHIP IN THE FUTURE

Now you have vital information that when applied with wisdom and experience, can advance your career. One of the goals for writing both *Creative Followership* and *Applied Creative Followership* is personal development.

Learning the Principles of Creative Followership increases the likelihood that you will apply them in your career. Now that you have an understanding of Creative Followership, start the next phase of your journey: become the author of the next ten Principles and beyond.

Ten empty Principle pages are included to encourage you to record the principles in the same format of the previous sections. Refer back to the notes you took as you worked your way through the material. Let these become Principles you create and implement during the continuous phase of becoming a successful Creative Follower.

False Assumption:

Creative Followership:

Principle:

Applied Creative Followership Notes:

False Assumption:

Creative Followership:

Principle:

Applied Creative Followership Notes:

False Assumption:

Creative Followership:

Principle:

Applied Creative Followership Notes:

False Assumption:

Creative Followership:

Principle:

Applied Creative Followership Notes:

False Assumption:

Creative Followership:

Principle:

Applied Creative Followership Notes:

False Assumption:

Creative Followership:

Principle:

Applied Creative Followership Notes:

False Assumption:

Creative Followership:

Principle:

Applied Creative Followership Notes:

False Assumption:

Creative Followership:

Principle:

Applied Creative Followership Notes:

False Assumption:

Creative Followership:

Principle:

Applied Creative Followership Notes:

False Assumption:

Creative Followership:

Principle:

Applied Creative Followership Notes:

ABOUT APPLIED CREATIVE FOLLOWERSHIP: A GUIDE TO BEGINNING YOUR JOURNEY

Applied Creative Followership: A Guide To Beginning Your Journey is a companion study to the book, Creative Followership: In the Shadow of Greatness by Jimmy Collins. This book may be used as a self-guided study for individuals, or as a discussion guide for groups. We want to assist as you begin to apply the Principles of Creative Followership to your life and career. We also want to encourage you to write your own Principles as you continue your journey and become a successful Creative Follower.

ABOUT CREATIVE FOLLOWERSHIP: IN THE SHADOW OF GREATNESS

Jimmy Collins delivers an inspiring message of everyone—from those just beginning their career to those who would like to reinvent themselves. He says, "My mission is to use my life experience to motivate others to venture out on a journey of discovery and adventure."

IS CREATIVE FOLLWERSHIP FOR YOU?

If you are just beginning in your career journey—yes!
If you want to restart your career journey—yes!
If you would like a better relationship with your boss—yes!
If you are ready to take on more responsibility—yes!

Jimmy used these principles to earn the trust of his boss Truett Cathy, founder and CEO of Chick-fil-A, Inc., which he claims resulted in Cathy's unwavering support and the recognition and reward that followed. These principles can be used by anyone, at any level of responsibility, in any organization. You could use them.

To find out more about Creative Followership, visit:
http://CreativeFollowership.com